VOLUME 2

The Sacred Gates

13 Original Rabbinic Parables
To Enter The Palace Of Wisdom

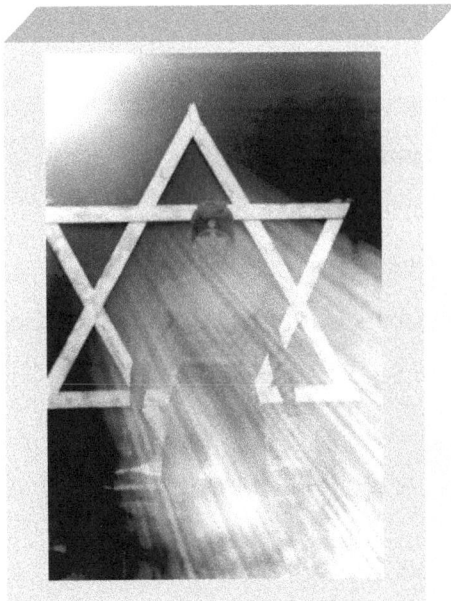

Child-Time Publishers

Established 1988

www.childtimepublishers.com

Library of Congress Number: 9780929934068

First Edition: January 2018

ISBN: 978-0-929934-06-8 (softcover)

Cover Art: Arlene Kingston

Logo Design: Sabina K. Mintz & Eric Sander Kingston

Photos Of Eric Sander Kingston By: William Kingston

Printed In USA

W.o.W.

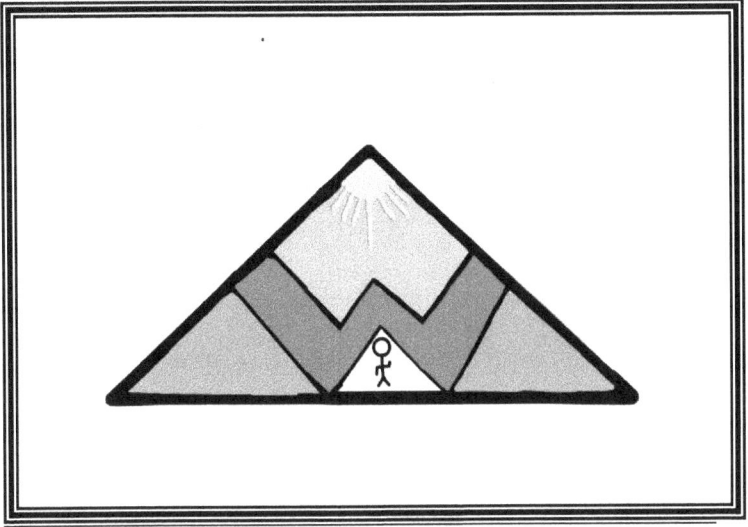

Wish On Wisdom ™

There was once a person, who was granted from Heaven, a wish. They could either wish for wealth, or wish for wisdom. The person replied: "I wish for wisdom. For through wisdom, I will attain great wealth."

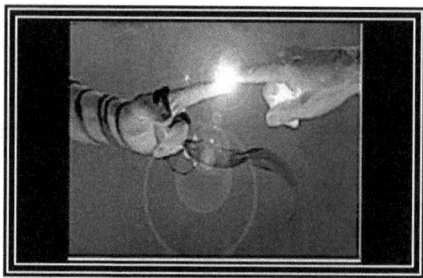

How To Use This Book

10 Power Prayer Of Divine Protection

1. May you surpass your teachers

2. May you go beyond yourself

3. May you leave a legacy of truth, love and justice

4. May you be an example of dignity

5. May your powers be used to unite all people, "not serve the vanity" of a single person

6. May you always be grateful for the smallest of things

7. May you never say "yes" when you mean "no"

8. May all your past hurts become the lessons that guide you towards your constructive destiny

9. May you see the greatest strength is within, when it connects constructively to others

And most of all

10. May you see, "The pain you feel is from the love you withhold."

Table Of Contents

The Holy Ones Among Us

A very old Rabbi, at the end of each of his teachings, would always go over and over the lives and hardships of the Holy Patriarchs and Matriarchs from the the Torah past. One day, one of his students asked him why he continued to go over and over, not just the teachings of these Sacred Texts, but of the hard reality of the lives of those who lived their wisdom. The student asked, "Isn't the basic knowledge more enough? Why must we hear, over and over again, the same story about these Holy People's hardships and struggles?" The Rabbi replied, "Because, someday you will no longer be students, and for your theoretic knowledge to become living wisdom, it has to be applied to life, and you need to understand LIFE IS NOT EASY FOR ANYONE!!! Not even, for the Holy Ones among us."

Insight: In reality, you will have your teachings tested FOR REAL.

Question: Where in your life can you learn to hold your beliefs in a more empowered way despite the reality of life?

Agreement: I,_____, agree and commit to, for myself, to understanding that reality will be the test of beliefs and learning.

Knowing Everything And A Heartfelt Wisdom

A Rabbi went to visit a man who closed himself to the world. This man had been trying for years, to know everything there was, before he went into action with his life. The Rabbi said to the man, "Before you were born, when you were a soul, you knew everything. When you are born, you do not remember, so you must learn again." The man said, "Yes!!! I am going to learn it all before I really step out into the world and make mistakes. I will learn it all before I am gone." The Rabbi said, "I see, but life is NOT about trying to be an island of perfection and knowing everything. It is about doing, and being part of something, imperfections and all. It is not just about the mind's knowledge. There is a wisdom of the heart that can only be learned by entering life as well." The Rabbi finally said, "One day, you will be gone. My friend, it is your life, so I will leave you with this, if you find one day that you know everything again, and that you have no earthly problems, and everything all around you is perfect, then you're already gone, for you're a soul back in Heaven." With that, the man opened his heart to that Higher heartfelt wisdom and stepped out into the world.

Insight: Life is about perfecting NOT attempting to be perfect.

Question: Where in your life can you have more faith in what you already (all ready) understand?

Agreement: I,_____, agree and commit to, for myself, to continuing to learn, but having faith in myself and understanding RIGHT NOW!

The Holy Dancer

There was once a man who danced with joy and brought much happiness to his world. One day, he fell into a deep sorrow, forgot himself and stopped dancing. He no longer felt the joy he used to feel and instead of looking at this as a passing part of his life, he transfixed upon it. Finally, he thought that he must find the Divine Presence to be restored again. He traveled very far, until he found a cave in which a great teacher Rabbi was living. It was rumored that this Rabbi had an answer for everything. The sad man approached and then asked, "Dear Rabbi, I am in great sorrow. I used to dance with joy, and now I only walk with misery, emptiness and sorrow. I am seeking the Divine Presence, for I understand She is full of happiness and joy. Do you know where She is?" The Rabbi looked at the sad man and then stated, "I know where She is NOT. She is not in your discontentment." The man looked at the Rabbi and then asked, "What does this mean?" The Rabbi said:

If you are not going to be happy
Be content with your misery

If you are not going to be full
Be content in your emptiness

If you are not going to be in joy
Be content in your sorrow

"But remember," said the Rabbi, "sorrow cannot drive out sorrow, only joy can do that, and as it is written in the Talmud: "The Divine Presence does not dwell where this no joy." With that, the man began to dance.

The Insight: Most times, it is our choice that makes us joyful, more so than the circumstance.

Question: Where in your life can you choose to be in a greater state of joy?

Agreement: I,_____, agree and commit to, for myself, to choosing a path of joy.

The Only One

One day, a very pompous man went to a Rabbi and asked, "If G-d is All Powerful, why can't He just do all things I need to accomplish for me?" The Rabbi said, "G-d works through people and with people. If, G-d did all things for us, what need would there be for us to exist? We must ALL do are parts with G-d in order to be an active part of His Creation!!! Are you so special, that you should be the only one?"

Insight: The greater our perspective, the more we understand we are not isolated and that working with the Divine is a choice.

Question: Where in your life can you widen your perspective to see struggles are a part of reality?

Agreement: I,_____, agree and commit to, for myself, to seeing the reality of my life as a part of developing creation we are must play a part in.

Faith, In The Fear That Never Falters

A student, who was no longer a child, was afraid of going to the next level of his life. He approached his Rabbi and asked him this question, "What is the difference between a person of fear and one who is afraid?" The student did not understand the difference. The Rabbi paused and then said, "Are you afraid of your own faith? Do you have fear of G-d's Power or are you afraid of Him?" The student still did not see the difference. Rabbi Joshua then said, "Moses would speak to the Children of Israel in the desert. He was G-d's "buffer" so-to-speak between the Children and direct communication with the Divine. When G-d spoke at the Mountain, directly to the Children of Israel they cried out, "Speak, to us Moses, and we will listen, but let not G-d Speak lest we die." They became afraid, mistrusting the Divine Power and their faith faltered. Then Moses, climbed the Mountain alone for G-d told him to keep the Children back. Yet, in his faith, as he climbed, he surely must have longed for all to ascend the Mountain, and if they remained faithful and trusted G-d despite their fear, they may have." The student then inquired, "Why did they not remain faithful?" The Rabbi answered, "Faith is understanding and fear, the "beginning of Wisdom is fear (awe) of G-d." The difference between being afraid and fear is this: To be afraid is to not really trust in the Power that guides and protects you. It is to refuse to let go and change evil ways, and to stay "stiff-necked" in your own ways. To have fear, the Divine fear, is to still be afraid, yet to keep going forward to the next level of your life with the ever expanding trust and understanding that everything is within G-d's Hands Whose Faith never falter's. So either," said the Rabbi, "You have Faith in that fear or you're afraid of your faith."

Insight: Don't let fear stop your from empowerment.

Question: Where in your life can you choose to keep moving forward despite your fear?

Agreement: I,_____, agree and commit to, for myself, to keeping my belief strong.

The Rock & Tears Of Moses

Adam and Eve sinned in the Garden and were expelled. Before leaving, they sat upon a Rock and wept tears of repentance for what had happened. The Rock filled with their tears from the wisdom they had gained through this loss. The Patriarch Jacob, wandered in the desert and laid his head down upon a Rock and said "This must be the place of G-d." The Rock filled with more Wisdom, like "waters that cover the sea." Many years later the Children of Israel thirsted in the desert as Moses led them. Thereupon, they came upon the Rock filled with "Water". G-d instructed Moses to speak to the Wisdom within the Rock, so that it may give forth Its Water. Moses was upset with the Children's stiff-neck way of being, and instead of speaking to the Rock, he struck it, and much of the "Water" disappeared. For this, Moses did not enter the Promised Land. G-d brought him to the Heavens, to atone. One day, he lay his head down, and in his sorrow he learned a great lesson, that the Promised Land is not only a place of state, but as much, a state of mind and a way of being. He realized, our every action is weighed and is important. He then wept and he wept great, great tears upon the place he laid his head down upon, upon the Rock he struck so many years before. Through his tears of Repentance, the Rock was refilled. One day, we will find this Rock and speak to It, and we will repair the tears of Moses, and the Rock shall open It's Wisdom up and Its Waters will flow and "Knowledge shall cover the earth as Water covers the sea" and our inner thirst, for the Divine, shall finally be quenched.

The Insight: One can always return to Divine Power for "The Gates of Tears are never closed."

Question: Where in your life can you learn a lesson from past mistakes and take back your power?

Agreement: I,_____, agree and commit to, for myself, to seeing my past as lessons.

Torah Wings

A young Rabbi went to his teacher, the senior Rabbi and asked, "It is said that when the great scholar Rabbi Akiva was alive, his intent caused the Torah to grow Wings. Rabbi, how does one grow wings for themselves and what were those Wings made of?" The senior Rabbi said, "My friend, make sure that through your life, you do many good deeds. Be a blessing to the world and for Israel." The young Rabbi said, "I will do and I will hear." Thereupon, the young Rabbi went out into the world and lived his life. Many, many years later he was at the end of his days. He lay in bed, and called out for assistance to save him. Suddenly his teacher, his Rabbi, came to him in a vision. The elder Rabbi stood next to his former student and in pointed up towards the Heavens, directing him where he should go when he passes. The former student Rabbi asked of his teacher, "It is a very great height! How am I going to get there? I would need very powerful wings to fly up that high."

The elder Rabbi said, "When you were young you, asked me how one grows wings and I told you good deeds. You see, as it is written in the Talmud when a man is about to pass, he calls out to his family, friends and even money to save him, but they cannot. Finally, it is his good deeds that come and say "We cannot save you, but we will be there, waiting for you on the other side. Your good deeds have created wings all through your life, and now they are the wings upon your back, waiting there to fly you up to Heaven!!!" With that, the man felt the Wings of Torah upon his back, in the form of the countless good deeds he had done. Then together, the two Rabbi's joined hands, as their Wings of Torah flew them to Heaven as One.

Insight: Never underestimate the power of good works.

Question: Where in your life can you contribute more with the understanding that it is cultivating your soul?

Agreement: I,_____, agree and commit to, for myself, to understanding that good deeds contribute to both worlds.

A Crown Of Humbleness

A man went to his Rabbi and throwing down his yamaka/head covering said, "Ah, it would be so good to have a crown and be a prince! Instead I have to struggle and remain humble as I serve G-d." "And what is the problem with humbleness and struggle?" said the Rabbi. "Sometimes, that is what it takes to fulfill our true and highest destiny." The man replied, "Moses was a prince! He was prince of all Egypt!" "Yes" replied the Rabbi, "Moses was a prince. He walked with the arrogant, the slave master and the sorcerers. Upon his head was the crown of arrogance, but he couldn't serve G-d, the people or truly fulfill his mission until he wore the crown of humbleness." "Yes" said the man, "I see that is true, but I wonder if Moses could have put the crown of that prince on once more, especially when the people were "stiff-necked and complaining," if he would have regretted turning away from being that prince." The Rabbi paused for a moment and then said, "Moses did put that crown of arrogance and pride on one more time and disobeyed G-d, the day he struck the rock in anger, and was forbidden, from that crown of pride, to enter the

Promised Land." The man humbly picked up his yamaka/head covering, and placed it like a crown of Light upon his head.

Insight: It's not only what someone wears upon their head, but what one is carrying in their heart that denotes their level of importance.

Question: Where in your life can you elevate prideful aspects?

Agreement: I,_____, agree and commit to, for myself, to seeing that divinity exists within.

A Key Is Just A Key

A Rabbi was given a key to a secret Palace of Wisdom. For years, he struggled to find this Divine Palace where he heard others gathered learning the secrets of the Universe. One day, he found the Palace. He approached Its vast golden door but it was locked tight. Finally, he pulled out the key he had carried for so many, many years, placed it in the lock and turned it. The golden door slowly opened. He entered and walked down a hallway. Echoing down the hallway, he heard in Its distance, a great gathering. As he approached the end of this hall, he beheld a powerful guard standing in front of a platinum door to a Divine Room filled with Light. He approached this vast door. He pulled his key out once again, but there was no visible lock. He showed his key to the guard, but the guard did not move. This went on for a while, until the Rabbi saw a box of keys to the side of him. He finally understood, the key was only valuable outside of the Palace. It was something EXTERNAL, only useful to get in. Dropping the key into the box, the guard stepped aside, and the Rabbi entered the Palace of Wisdom.

Insight: The compass and the map are NOT the treasure.

Question: Where in your life do you believe the externals are more important than the internals?

Agreement: I,_____, agree and commit to, for myself, to seeing the locked door to enter is the self.

Dirty Paper & Brick

One day, an arrogant man stood before the Judgement of G-d. Next to this arrogant man, stood a small humble man. G-d then said them, "Look down at your feet." They did. "What do you see?" asked G-d. Both replied, "We see an ant." They watched, as the ant carried an object ten times its own weight. Something neither of them could do. G-d asked, "What do you think?" The arrogant man, rose up his leg and was about to crush the ant with the soul of his foot. When G-d said, "Be careful." The man's foot hovered for over the ant. G-d then said, "Step forward." The arrogant man, pushed the other out of the way and stepped forward. G-d asked, "Why do you do such a thing!" The arrogant man said, "I knew this man on earth! I had ten times his wealth and ten times the size of his home!" G-d said, "Let me get this straight. You had more pieces of dirty paper, you call money and you had more bricks, creating a bigger house, than the man next to you and therefore you are proud and boisterous here!" There was a moment's pause, as the arrogant man saw the Soul of Heaven raise up and hover above his head.

Insight: Arrogance creates the loss of perspective towards power.

Question: Where in your life can you see others more equally?

Agreement: I,_____, agree and commit to, for myself, to being more humble when dealing others.

Dirty Paper

One day, two souls who both had miserable lives of poverty upon the earth, were complaining to each other. Each was trying to prove it suffered more. Thereupon, a ministering Angel appeared before them from the Courts of Heaven. "Both of you," said the Angel, "were once very, very wealthy for a while, and both of you lost much of your fortunes because of your wicked ways. Your once great prides would not let either of you see the truth before your eyes. Your anger blinded you to the point, where you could not see how you came across your fortune, or how you lost it, or Who was truly the reason of why you had the fortune in the first place. We, the Divine Courts, are sending you both back to earth to see if you have learned to overcome your blinding arrogance!" In one second, both souls were in bodies upon the face of the earth. For a punishment, they were sent to a desolate town as street janitors, with one mission: to clean up a mountain of dirty paper that blocked a street and deal with its disposal in any way they chose. They were told that if they cleaned the street properly, they would be free from their poverty. Each was placed on opposite sides of this paper mountain. The first man, was still enraged, especially when he saw this mountain of dirty paper before him. He went about his mission, angry, confused and blinded by feeling betrayed, now by even Heaven. The first man, finally just ran away and hid in some desolate part of the town. The second man, went about his mission with joy and love, having learned his lesson and sweeping up the mountain of $100 dollar bills that Heaven was before him.

Insight: Self-absorbed anger always blocks perspective and understanding of that which is around us.

Question: Where in your life is anger obscuring your powers of insight and choice?

Agreement: I,_____, agree and commit to, for myself, to

A Second First Wish

It was the birthday of a very learned Rabbi who was now entering into his forties. He was thinking about the brevity of life when suddenly the Divine appeared before him. The Divine said, "It is your birthday. I Am here to grant you a wish. What would you like?" The Rabbi thought for a moment and then asked the Divine, "What is 40 years to You?" The Divine said, "Forty years to Me is nothing." Then the Rabbi asked, "What is 120 years like to You?" The Divine replied, "120 years to Me is like one second." "Ok," said the Rabbi, "Then, for my birthday wish I would like one second."

Insight: Make sure you use your wisdom and understand what you are being offered before you answer.

Question: Where in your life could your wisdom bring you greater rewards?

Agreement: I,_____, agree and commit to, for myself, to utilizing the opportunities life brings my way.

A Single Dollar And A Single Hour

There was once a Rabbi who was always trying to get one of his congregants, an investment banker, to study just one more hour a week of Yiddishkeit (Torah Learning). The man would not commit to this, saying he did not wish to invest the time. He was always concerned with the returns he would get on money or time. Often, he would just replay to the Rabbi, "How can one hour really make a difference?" The Rabbi, would reply back, "Anything can make a difference; even a single dollar can make difference." "How so?" replied the banker. He then said that he represented a lucrative bank and dealt with millions of dollars each day. One day, the Rabbi saw this banker purchasing a lottery ticket. The Rabbi approached the banker, and asked him why he was purchasing such a thing when the odds against winning where very small. The banker said, "It's a great, possible, future return for a small investment now." "I see" said the Rabbi "and how much does the lottery ticket cost?" The man replied, "A single dollar. I purchase one ticket each week." The Rabbi said, "A single dollar, or even a single hour, can certainly return much." With that, the man committed to the weekly hour of study.

Intention: Investment of study, yields the return of greater wealth of wisdom.

Question: Where could you be expanding your education by investing a little more time in it?

Agreement: I,_____, agree and commit to, for myself, to furthering my development and education.

ACKNOWLEDGEMENTS

I would like to thank my mother & father, William & Arlene Kingston, as well as my sister, Wendy & her husband Eric S. Mintz & my nieces Sabina & Juliet.

The Love Between You

Written For

My Father Mother,
William & Arlene Kingston

The Love Between You

One day,

Two soul-mates who had spent a whole lifetime together

Were going over the events of their lives.

As they looked over their many struggles and hardships,

They noticed that during their worst moments

It seemed that it was only each other

That pulled the other through,

It seemed that it was only their togetherness and faith

That held their lives together.

One day the L-rd appeared before them and they asked,

"L-rd, during our worst trials and tribulations

It seems it was only our togetherness

That held our lives together,

It seemed was only our togetherness

That kept our faith alive,

Where in all this was the Presence of G-d?"

The L-rd replied: "My precious children,

My beautiful Creations

I

Was the love between you"

ABOUT ERIC

Eric Sander Kingston is a master strategist, martial artist and composer. Best known for rapid transformational techniques, Eric uses a specifically created system of strategic drills, martial arts, original writings, to transfer specific techniques, and practical tools, to his clients. Eric's system empowers people to breakthrough their fear, and cultivate a deep, internal power of awareness, allowing them greater access to achieve their goals, and cultivate a life of stability and sustainable success.

Connect with Eric directly, for personal, or group, training, consultation, custom written works, or to have Eric personally transform your corporation or event, visit:

www.ericsanderkingston.com

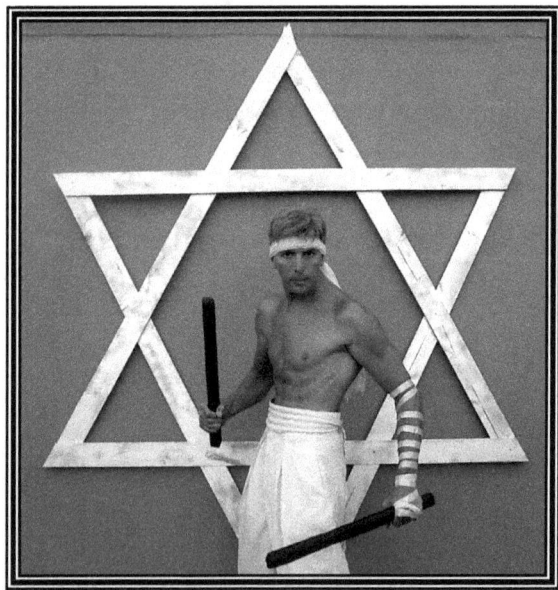

Wish On Wisdom Philosophy

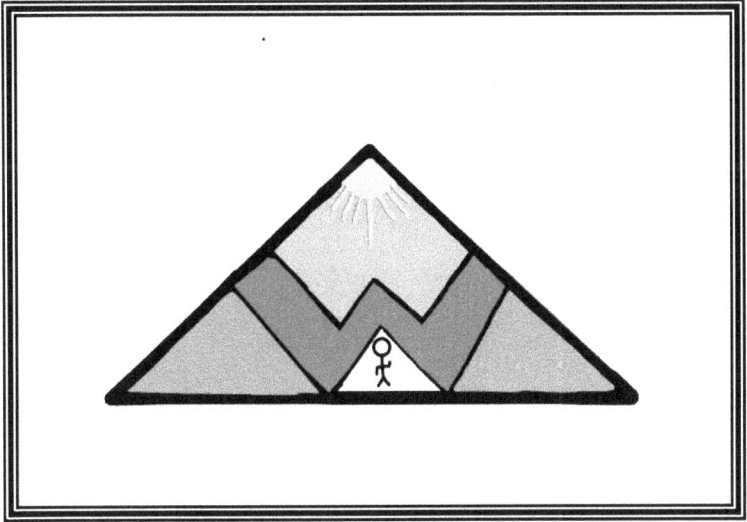

Every race, religion and region has great wisdom to offer humanity. The Wish On Wisdom parables seek to impart this wisdom to create bridges of unity between all peoples of our planet earth.

www.wishonwisdom.com

"The world is a narrow bridge,
the main thing is not to be afraid."
Rabbi Nachman of Breslov

OTHER PUBLICATIONS
BY CHILD-TIME PUBLISHERS:

Established 1988

www.childtimepublishers.com

THE SACRED GATE

VOLUME 1

13 Original Rabbinic Parables
To Enter The Palace Of Wisdom

The 13 Original Rabbinic Parables within this book are meant to be flexible, practical and interactive. The parables teach universal wisdom's applicable, through the readers interpretation, to any race, religion or region. Each parable concludes with an Insight, Question and Agreement, one can choose to use for further spiritual development.

For other Original Parable Books see:

wishonwisdom.com

THE PRIMORDIAL WAY
Strategies To Inner Self Mastery
Written By Eric Sander Kingston

Eric Sander Kingston's newest book on internal strategy & philosophy of inner conflict to achieve non-duality and start transforming inner fears.

Please Note: This book is NOT intended for beginners who do not have some background in ancient energy literature, conflict resolution based on transformation towards inner mutual understanding or for Martial Artists who do not grasp Gandhi's Wisdom: *"The greatest demons in the world are those running around our own hearts."*

"It does not matter how many men you defeat! If you do not conquer your inner demons, you will pass your demons onto your child as your parent passed theirs onto you."

From the Film Dragon

The Primordial Way

Strategies To Inner Self Mastery

By Master Strategist
Eric Sander Kingston

AFRICAN WOMEN'S WISDOM

Original Parables
Based On The Proverbs Of Africa
To Empower The Feminine
Written By Eric Sander Kingston

Original one paragraph Parables with an interactive edge designed for personal power and transformation based upon the wisdom of African culture.

African Women's Wisdom

Original Parables
Based On The Proverbs Of
Africa

By Eric Sander Kingston

THE HIDDEN DOOR
26 Original Rabbinic Parables
To Reveal The Concealed

26 Original Rabbinic Parables with an interactive edge designed for personal power and transformation..

The Hidden Door

26 Original Rabbinic Parables
To Reveal The Concealed

Eric Sander Kingston

Co-Author Steve L. Cohn

The Bagels Are Coming!

A Humorous Look At How Bagels Bring Peace To The World.

Written and Illustrated by Arlene Kingston

Paperback,

Library Of Congress Number: 88-63105

ISBN: 0-929934-00-8
ISBN: 0-929934-00-8

A HUMOROUS LOOK AT HOW BAGELS BRING PEACE TO THE WORLD

THE BAGELS ARE COMING!

by arlene Kingston

NOTES